FIRST LESSONS NATIVE AMERICAN FLUTE: HOW TO SIT ON A ROCK

BY ANDREW MARKUS BISHKO

ILLUSTRATIONS BY TOM MCCUNE

Online Audio   www.melbay.com/22195BCDEB

AUDIO CONTENTS

1 2 3 4 5 6 7 8 9 0

Visit us on the Web at www.melbay.com — E-mail us at email@melbay.com

CONTENTS

GRATITUDE

MY FAMILY:
RACHAEL, HONOR, JOYOUS, SHEPHERD
& THOSE WHO ARE COMING

MY PARENTS FOR MUSIC LESSONS

CRAZY COYOTE

NEAL MARTIN

THE ALASKA FLUTE CIRCLE

THE NEW ENGLAND CONSERVATORY

BRUCE AND CONNIE COMPTON &
THE COMMUNITY OF LIGHT

MICHELLE

BIG MITCH

LITTLE CROW—THE GIFT OF COMMUNICATION

ONE WHO WALKS WITH BIRDS—THE GIFT OF RESPECT

WEE-HAUK-TAW—THE GIFT OF MAGIC

LUDWIG VAN BEETHOVEN—
THE GIFT OF JOY, WHICH IS THE CENTER

MOTHER AND FATHER IN HEAVEN & EARTH

MY SELF FOR COMMITTING TO THE PATH OF
SPIRITUAL GROWTH & TRANSFORMATION

INTRODUCTION

WHY THIS BOOK IS DIFFERENT

Several wonderful method books are available for learning the Native American Flute. Most of these follow the standard approach for learning instruments found throughout the western world: a few basic instructions on techniques followed by notated songs composed or passed on through tradition. The student twists his or her fingers to match to match the squiggles on the page, hoping to hear the "right" notes. This effort is well rewarded with the great satisfaction of playing several good tunes in short order.

While this approach has great benefits, as centuries of brilliant western classical musicians can attest, I find it to be almost antithetical to the heart of the Native American Flute tradition. Many traditional tales describe the inception of the Flute as a profoundly personal experience. The Flutes were measured by the length of a man's arm and finger holes placed where his fingers fell, producing an individual scale with unique intonation. They were most often used for courtship, expressing and sharing the idiosyncratic essence of a man's spirit as he laid his soul bare before his intended bride.

So what is the alternative for today's NAF neophyte? New owners of the Native American Flute have often been told to go "sit on a rock" and teach themselves how to play.

Andrew Markus Bishko Sitting on a Rock

This is great advice! New Flutists with a sense of adventure make great discoveries, and are surprised at the beauty of the music that so quickly develops from their explorations.

Yet in my years of teaching, I have discovered that the initial glow often wears off. Enthusiastic explorations become repetitive meanderings in the doldrums, with no guidance as to how to navigate back to the swiftly flowing currents of creativity. That is where this book comes in.

HOW TO USE THIS BOOK:

I have found the simple lessons contained within this book to be endlessly inspiring. After 45 years of playing musical instruments, I still return to these ideas to create anew.

The lessons in this book are arranged in order to draw you into your own world of melody. I based this order on what I have observed with my students. You may read through all of the lessons before you begin: some of the lessons will appeal to you now, others maybe in ten years, maybe never. You may stay with a lesson for a day or a year. The journey is your own: follow your intuition and choose the pages in this book in the order that will best serve you.

For example, I began my Native American Flute journey with the radically playful approach outlined in *Lesson 6*, but I find that most of my students benefit from first grounding in the serenity of the traditional scale taught in *Lesson 1*.

I advise dividing your sessions with the Flute into three stages of practice:
1. Start by playing and experimenting with whatever you like. This is like the babbling of the baby learning how to talk. When you run out of time or ideas, move to stage 2.
2. Disciplined practice of the exercises: This is like the child learning the ABCs.
3. Forget about the exercises and create new music! This is the teenager dexterously texting her friends…

Each chapter is divided into four directions, to follow the cycle of learning. The sun rises in the East, initiates a new day and inspires new ideas. It travels across the South as we put these ideas into practice and make them a part of our lives. As the sun sets in the West, these practices are fully integrated and transformed as we have added them to ourselves. As we sleep at night, our learning is assimilated in the North …

Note: This book is written with the 6 hole flute in mind, but can easily be adapted to the 7, 5 or 4 hole flutes by adding or subtracting fingers.

NOTES ON THE CD

The accompanying CD contains specific instructional examples of the exercises in the text interspersed with improvised performances. The tracks are represented in the text by a black diamond with a number inside, for example:

All the recordings were made on my flame juniper Flute in "G", pictured in the cover photo. For most of the tracks I set up my MacBook, Mbox, and microphone next to my open kitchen window and recorded without any effects or additional processing, accompanied by whatever birds, breezes, bugs, and frogs happened by.

In my experience, the Flute in the key of G is a popular size for beginners. If your flute is in a different key, your fingerings will not produce the same notes as you hear on the CD, although the notes on each flute will relate to each other the same way. (See *Lesson 5: South "Key Ideas"* for more information.)

The CD is intended to inspire, and to offer direction and example. The whole point of this book is to sound like yourself, so if you don't sound like the CD that's perfectly fine!

ᶦ Note: swap North and South if you live in the Southern Hemisphere

A BRIEF INTRODUCTION TO THE MUSICAL NOTATION USED IN THIS BOOK

The intention of this book is to discover and express the music within your self. Accordingly, there are no written, pre-composed pieces of music for you to learn. There are, however, several exercises that are best communicated through musical notation. This book uses the two most popular ways of notating music for the Native American Flute:

Fingering diagrams

Fingering diagrams are used throughout this book whenever musical notation is required. These diagrams offer a direct illustration of the Flute, which holes are covered by the fingers and which are uncovered. They are great for indicating which note to play, but don't show how long or short to play it, whether to play it soft or loud, etc. This is sufficient for many Flute players, who rely heavily on their ears and personal choices for rhythms, dynamics, and expression.

Nakai TAB

For those interested in greater precision, the great pioneer of the Native American Flute Revival, R. Carlos Nakai, has devised an ingenious adaptation of the Western Classical music notation system, known as Nakai Tablature, or "Nakai Tab." This looks just like western notation, with all the advantages of precise rhythmic notation, articulation, expressive, and dynamic markings. The difference is that the lines and spaces on the staff represent fingerings rather than pitches.

That means that the same music can be played by any Flute in any key. However, the actual pitches (known as "concert pitch"—the notes you would find on the piano) will vary according to the size, or "key" of the flute. In Western terms, the lowest note of this system is called "F Sharp", which means that the pitches will only match the concert pitches if you are playing an F Sharp (F♯) Flute.

All the information you need is provided in the fingering diagrams and accompanying explanations. And for those readers familiar with music reading, and those who would like to learn, I have included Nakai TAB notation along with the fingering charts.

Whenever the fingering diagrams are used together with Nakai TAB, I have used Clint Goss' NAFTracks 6 hole Font (www.flutopedia.com).

Here is an example of how I will use notation in this book:

THE TRADITIONAL SCALE IN FINGERING DIAGRAMS AND NAKAI TAB

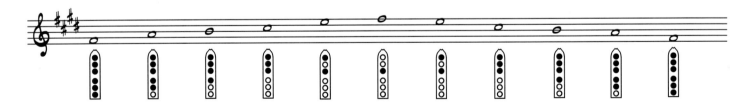

LESSON 1: HANDS

Silence. A haunting sound wafts through the crisp dawn air. Your ears reach out to embrace this beauty. Stalking the melody with the hunger of a wolf, your eyes catch sight of a mysterious stranger, face hidden in the shadows. A magic wand of extraordinary beauty rests on the hidden lips and floats in the air in front of him. His fingers dance across the Flute, seeming to evoke a sound at once wholly of Mother Earth and wholly of Father Sky. Without even realizing it, your hands have been reaching for the Flute. The Master brings his melody to a gentle close, and places the Flute in your outstretched hands. You stare in wonder and disbelief at the great gift you have received.

Within minutes of entering my music teaching studio, new students invariably point to my Native American Flutes and ask, "What's that?" Lovingly hand carved out of beautiful natural materials, the Flutes are extraordinarily beautiful to look at, and any reader of this book will know that it's hard to keep your hands off of them!

While the sound begins with the breath (see *Lesson 2*), the new Flutist's first question is, "Where do I put my fingers?" So I will begin with the hands, and restrict my present comments on the breath to the traditional, "Blow in the pointy end."

EAST: INITIATION

PLACING FINGERS ON THE FLUTE

Figure this out quickly, and then go immediately to the Playing Position exercise.

Hold the flute with the "pointy end" towards you, holes on top. Put your thumbs underneath the flute, left hand closer to you, and gently place your left index finger, middle finger, and ring finger over the top three holes (top two on a five-hole flute, and similarly with your right hand. (If you have a five hole flute, simply ignore hole 3 here and throughout the book).

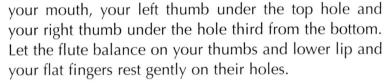

Place your fingers **flatly** across the holes. Most western instruments (pianos, violins, classical flutes, guitars…) are played with curved fingers. You will have much better hole coverage and subtlety of movement on the Native American Flute with flat fingers.

PLAYING POSITION

Imagine a string attached to the top of your head and running up into heaven. As you breathe gently and deeply, feel that string gently pulling you upward as you stand or sit tall.

Now, place the "pointy end" in your mouth, your left thumb under the top hole and your right thumb under the hole third from the bottom. Let the flute balance on your thumbs and lower lip and your flat fingers rest gently on their holes.

Maintain relaxed shoulders and arms as you raise and lower the flute, finding the range of balance points where you can lift your fingers and balance the flute on your thumbs. As you feel more comfortable and courageous, try raising your fingers up and wiggling them; letting the flute float on the thumbs and the lower lip.

Many beginners try to hold the flute vertically, and grip it with the fingers to keep it from slipping. This may produce a good "photo op," but it restricts the free wiggling of the fingers by giving them extra responsibility that they just don't need. The vertical position also closes up the chest, breath, and heart (see *Lessons 2* and *8*).

BLOW ALREADY!

If you have followed the previous instructions scrupulously and resisted the urge to blow into your flute and begin making music, you may consider yourself a model of discipline and self-restraint: consider a career as a prison warden. You may now blow into your flute and wiggle your fingers and have a great time!

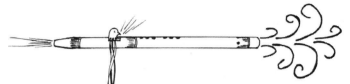

If you rushed through the instructions and began enchanting yourself with the beautiful (or not so beautiful) sounds produced by your blowing and wiggling, go back to the beginning of the East section of this chapter, relax, and enjoy the exercises.

Now that we're all on the same page, get your best playing position going. Feel the flute floating lightly on your thumbs and lower lip, as if it were held by another Heavenly String. Blow gently into the blowhole, and imagine that the flute is floating, suspended on the gentle breeze of air streaming from your lungs. Ahhhhh.

SOUTH: PRACTICE
LOW TO HIGH, HIGH TO LOW

Sound is vibration: the faster the vibration, the higher the pitch. Small things tend to vibrate faster than big things, as any parent of small children can attest!

We make our flute "bigger" and longer by covering the holes sequentially from the top—the hole closest to the pointy end—to the bottom.

Assume your best playing position. Now lay your index, middle, and ring finger (henceforth known as fingers 1, 2, & 3) flat across the top three holes.

Blow gently, and listen. Then lift finger 3 and blow again for a slightly higher pitch. Lift finger 2 and repeat, then lift finger 1, balancing the flute on your thumbs, and repeat.

After you can play each of these notes one at a time, try lifting the fingers up 3-2-1 all in one breath.

When you have mastered lifting up, start with all fingers up and place the fingers down sequentially, 1-2-3.

Then play around with going up and down.

Make sure that you are covering the holes completely, hold down 1, 2, & 3, and repeat the exercise with the fingers of the right hand, now known as 4, 5, & 6, sequentially.

 Keep your attention on closing the holes completely with your fingers. Now play with 6-5-4-3-2-1, 1-2-3-4-5-6.

7 You may notice that the sequence of notes produced on the six hole Flute by this exercise sounds a little strange. To find out why, go West!

SQUAWK!

Squeaks and squawks are usually due to incomplete hole coverage. Most beginners pull the Flute away and look at it oddly, as if to say, "How dare you squawk at me!" Well, brothers and sisters, don't blame the Flute! Flatten those fingers, especially the middle fingers on each hand.

You will eventually learn to feel whether your hole is covered or not. To accelerate this process, **slowly** add one finger at a time, alternating back and forth. Repeat each example as necessary, adding fingers progressively down the flute:

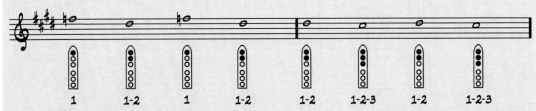

| 1 | 1-2 | 1 | 1-2 | 1-2 | 1-2-3 | 1-2 | 1-2-3 |

Note that I have begun to use Nakai TAB along with the fingering diagrams. See the Introduction for more explanation.

Another source of unsatisfying sounds may be the placement of the block. See *Appendix: Flute Anatomy, Care, and Troubleshooting.*

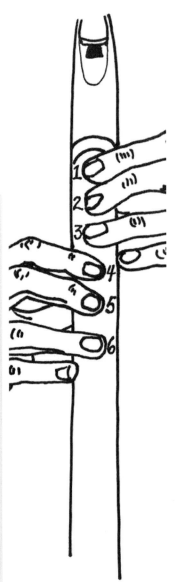

WEST: TRANSFORMATION

THE TRADITIONAL SCALE

A scale is a set of pitches (a.k.a. tones: sounds of a determined frequency of vibration) from which we choose to form melodies. Different types of scales exhibit different patterns of energy between the tones, and produce melodies of differing characters.

For example, the most common scale in Western music is called the "Major Scale" –the old "do-re-mi-fa-so-la-ti-do." This scale gives the raw materials for cheery, uplifting melodies from "Mary Had A Little Lamb" to "Ode to Joy" and "Amazing Grace." Another common Western scale is the "Minor Scale," which produces intense melodies like "When Joshua fought the battle of Jericho" and "Let My People Go."

The most common scale for the Native American Flute is known in music theory terms as the "Minor Pentatonic Scale." It is related to the Western Minor Scale, but has five tones ("pentatonic") instead of the seven found in Western scales. **8**

Here is the fingering (along with Nakai TAB notation) for the Traditional Scale:

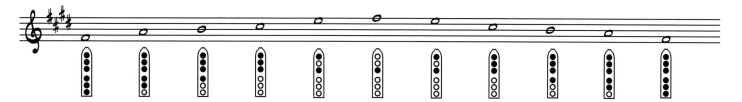

WHY ARE THERE 6 TONES IN THE 5-TONE SCALE?

Play the lowest and highest tones in the scale. The highest is vibrating exactly twice as fast as the lowest, and is given the same name in Western music. A scale consists of the tones that span this interval, known as an "octave." Western music counts the number of differing tones in the scale, so the repeated octave doesn't "count." On instruments with a wider range of pitches, such as the silver flute or the piano, the scale can be repeated in higher and lower octaves.

Note that the ring finger of the left hand (finger 3 on the diagram) doesn't move. Many traditional 5-hole Flutes omit this hole entirely. Most modern Native American Flutes employ this hole in a variety of "cross fingerings" to produce the tones in between the notes of the traditional scale.

Play the scale from the lowest to the highest tone and back down. The traditional scale alone transforms with its heartful melody!

11

NORTH: WISDOM

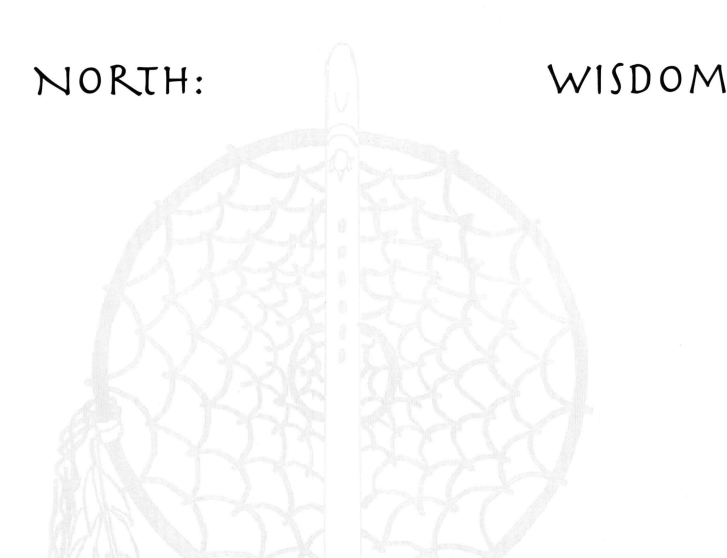

CREATING MELODIES

Now admit it: as soon as you got your fingers on the flute, you got your nose out of this book and started creating music! It was fun for a while, but certain notes didn't seem to "fit." Go on back to Low to High, High to Low and The Traditional Scale.

The Master beckons towards a well-worn ancient rock, spotted with lichens. You sit there, both comforted and energized by its solidity. Freely explore the notes of the traditional scale, going up, going down, and skipping around. Make these notes a part of yourself. Melodies will begin to form, wander off, and re-form. Journal your experiences on the Dreamcatcher. When you find the inspiration waning, journey on to *Lesson 2*.

LESSON 2:
BREATH AND TONE

Enchanted by the harmony of the five tones, you close your eyes and follow the wandering melody to the end of your breath. Open your eyes and listen. The warm wind of early spring rustles through the dry oak leaves remaining on the trees. Green buds open into tender understory leaves and flowers, waving softly in the gentle breeze. As your senses follow the eddying currents of air, you perceive an inner rustling. Placing the Flute to your lips once more, your improvisations seem to have lost the luster of those first explorations. You gaze down at the beautiful instrument in your hand and ask, "Is that all there is?"

The spring breeze teaches us that Breath is the life of our bodies. With this same Breath, we breathe life into the Flute. Now that our fingers have had their fun and settled in, let us learn to create the sound that first drew us to this journey.

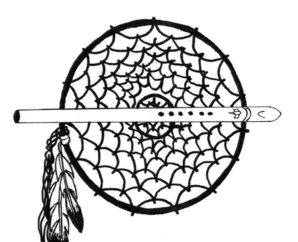

EAST: INITIATION

HOW TO BREATHE DEEPLY

Inhale!

Find a full-length mirror or a willing observer. Take a deep, deep breath. What part of your body is expanding? Many of you will see your ribs expand and shoulders rise. This is a diagram of your lungs.

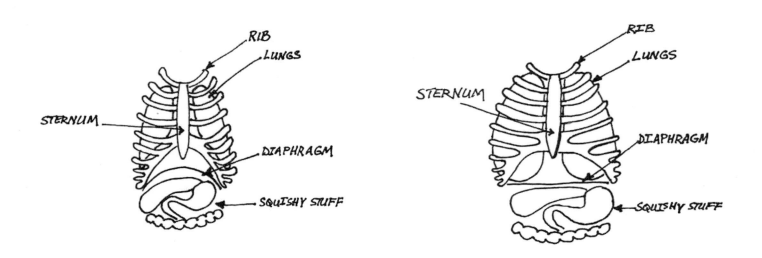

The lungs can expand in all directions, and our ribs are hinged to allow for this expansion into the chest cavity. This is quite sufficient for the shallow, everyday breathing required by most tasks. But our lung capacity is far greater than that cage of bones will allow.

Notice the curved line at the bottom of the diagram, labeled diaphragm (pronounced "di'-uh-fram"). This enormous muscle runs from one side to the other and front to back of the body, completely dividing the top half, which houses the lungs, heart, and very few other glands and organs, from the bottom half, which contains the stomach, intestines, liver, pancreas, and many other internal organs—all of which I have labeled "Squishy Stuff." The weird thing about the diaphragm is that it contains no sensory nerves of its own—we cannot normally experience and control it directly. In order to make use of this great resource, we learn to sense it by how it affects other parts of the body that we can feel.

When we inhale and contract the diaphragm, flattening it out, we create a large empty volume into which our lungs happily expand, filling with life-giving oxygen. This flattening pushes down against the "squishy stuff," causing our tummies to expand outward. We may even feel pressure in our lower back as the squishy stuff retreats from the advancing diaphragm.

The diaphragm helps to move fluids and tone organs throughout the body. Increasing its movement can have profound health benefits.

We can practice Diaphragm Breathing by lying on our backs, knees bent, with a book balanced on our bellies:

Inhale deeply, and direct your breath to raise the book.

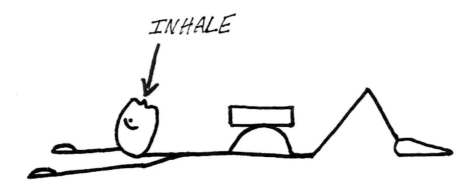

Exhale slowly, like blowing a note on the Flute, and let the book drop.

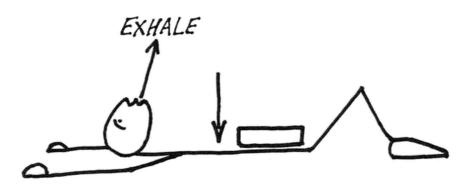

You may find at first that you are raising the book with your abdominal muscles instead, or that the book rises on the exhale rather than the inhale. Keep trying to match the book's rise with the inhale, and you will begin to sense the action of the diaphragm.

Now let's try this standing up. Stand with your feet flat on the earth, shoulder-width apart. Make sure that you do not have your knees locked back.

Locking the knees creates a chain reaction in the thigh muscles, which press up against the abdominals and inhibit the free motion of the diaphragm. If you're not convinced, ask someone to give you a gentle push as you lock your knees, and then with knees slightly flexed. Knee locking is part of the fight-or-flight response, and who

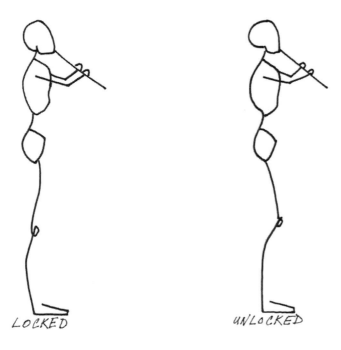

LOCKED   UNLOCKED

wants that?? If you've been locking your knees most of your life, your freed knees will seem weak and wobbly at first, but you will soon be feeling stronger and happier. Amen.

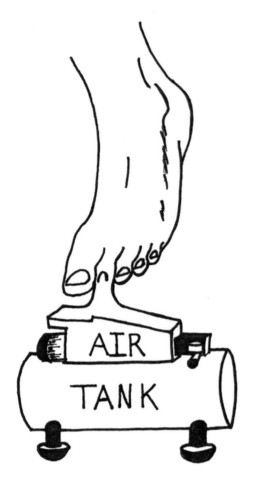

Ok, enough of my knee-jerk sermon. Now, put your hand on your tummy and breathe the same way as you mastered with the tummy book exercise. Directing the air downward into the diaphragm rather than outward into the ribs may seem awkward at first. I like to visualize air tanks in my legs, or, even better, attached to my toes and heels. For some reason, the second toe next to the big toe produces the best results for me.

Imagine yourself filling these air tanks and soon you will have a clear understanding of how to direct air throughout your lungs and expand them to their maximum potential.

Exhale!
We now know more about bringing the breath into the body. Breathing this way will in itself expand the resonance of your body, producing a richer Flute tone. There is one more aspect of breath control to complete before we move on to our discussion of tone.

Breathe in, a deep diaphragm breath. Blow a long, soft note on your Flute, to the end of your breath.

Did it feel at the beginning of your note that your lungs were bursting to release the air? Did the initial airstream rush out like water over a dam?

It is quite possible to have greater and greater control over this flow. I like to visualize my full lungs as a jar of honey. A slight tip of the jar allows a smooth, steady stream of air to flow gently into my Flute. The sensation in the lungs transforms from one of uncomfortable pressure to pleasurable fullness.

Now let's direct this precious resource in the production of a beautiful Flute tone.

TONE

The word "Tone" may refer to an individual pitch, or the specific quality of the musical sound, as in "Tone Color."

Where does the sound of the Flute come from? Sit or stand in your best playing position (see *Lesson 1*). Make sure that you are holding the Flute horizontally to open up the arms and chest. Close your eyes, take a deep breath into your diaphragm, blow one long note, and listen. Where does the sound come from? Repeat this until you have a very clear idea of this location. Trust your perception—there are no "wrong" answers.

Many students locate the sound somewhere above the end of the block.

This is where the vibration is actually set up. The air is focused under the block into a thin, fast moving stream, which splits across the sharp edge of the hole, which produces a consistently vibrating pressure wave in the air column inside the Flute. (See *Appendix*) Unlike transverse flutes (such as the Western classical flute), recorder, panpipes, or any other world flute that I know of, the first air chamber of the Native American Flute distances the vibrating edge from the head of the flutist.

Every musical instrument consists of a mechanism for setting up the vibration, and a body for molding and shaping that vibration into the desired tone. Pluck a guitar string, and the vibration resonates through the big wooden box. Strike the skin of a drum and the vibration resonates through its cylindrical body. Press the key of an electronic keyboard and send a signal to the paper cone of its speaker, which is converted to the desired sound vibration. The turbulence set up at the sharp edge downwind of the Flute's block resonates through the lovingly carved and lacquered body of the Flute, which molds and shapes the raw vibration into the luscious tone that we desire.

But the Flute cannot sing by itself: it doesn't work unless we attach it to a human body. And that body, too, resonates, molds and shapes the tone.

SOUTH: PRACTICE

Close your eyes. Imagine, if you will, a planet far off in space, host to an exquisite alien civilization. The loving inhabitants of planet Fluto have long left the language of words behind. Instead, when the Flutonians open their mouths to speak, the air is filled with rich Flute-like tones.

Now you be the Flutonian: return to your best playing position (see *Lesson 1*). Close your eyes, and pretend there is no Flute before you. All that remains is your body and the desire to use that body to express your spirit. Breathe deeply into your diaphragm, blow one long note after another, to the end of your breath, and listen. With your mind, move the location of the sound generation into your own throat, feeling the vibration within your own body. The back of your mouth and throat open wide, as if for a yawn, creating a warm resonant cavern for the sound to inhabit. You may find the sound traveling beyond your throat, vibrating in any part of your body. Let this happen, take note of your experiences and the tonal variations produced.

Perhaps the Flutonian exercise was a truly alien experience for you. Do not be discouraged! The very thought of connecting the body to the Flute in partnership often produces a dramatic increase in the beauty of the tone. With time you will learn to feel and master this beauty. Repeat this exercise as often as you like—it's especially effective just before bedtime. Journal your discoveries and go West to transform them…

WEST: TRANSFORMATION

VIBRATO

As you gain more control over your breath and tone, you may wish to explore vibrato—a pulsating variation of pitch (moving between slightly higher and lower) and amplitude (moving between louder and softer). This effect, most likely borrowed from vocal performance, is common to many instruments and musical cultures throughout the world. Classical violinists, for example, will shake their hands to produce miniscule variations in the pitch of their instruments.

The Flutist, like the vocalist, may produce vibrato through the pulsation of the muscles inside the body—most notably our oddly spelled friend, the diaphragm.

Begin with a deep diaphragm breath. Now give a big Santa Claus laugh, HO HO HO, sharply pulsing the diaphragm on each HO. Hold your hand a foot or two in front of your mouth, repeating the exercise without the "HO" sound and feel the warm pulses of air on your palm.

Now breathe again, and place the Flute on your lips. Use your diaphragm to pulse "ho" breaths into your Flute. At first, each ho will be a separate note. Now allow the breath to flow in between the pulses. Relax the "ho" pulsations now to different levels, exploring the possibilities.

Once you have some control of pulsing the sound with your diaphragm, play through the traditional scale, up and down, pulsing each note. Begin with six very slow pulses per note. Really hold yourself back and control them. Experiment with deeper and shallower pulses. Then, very gradually increase the speed of the pulses, gaining control of all the variations of vibrato speed. Repeat the exercise with anywhere from 2 to 9 pulses per note, at varying speeds.

Be patient and persistent in this exercise and you will master a tremendous range of expressive vibratos, not to mention tremendous health benefits and abs of steel!

NORTH: WISDOM

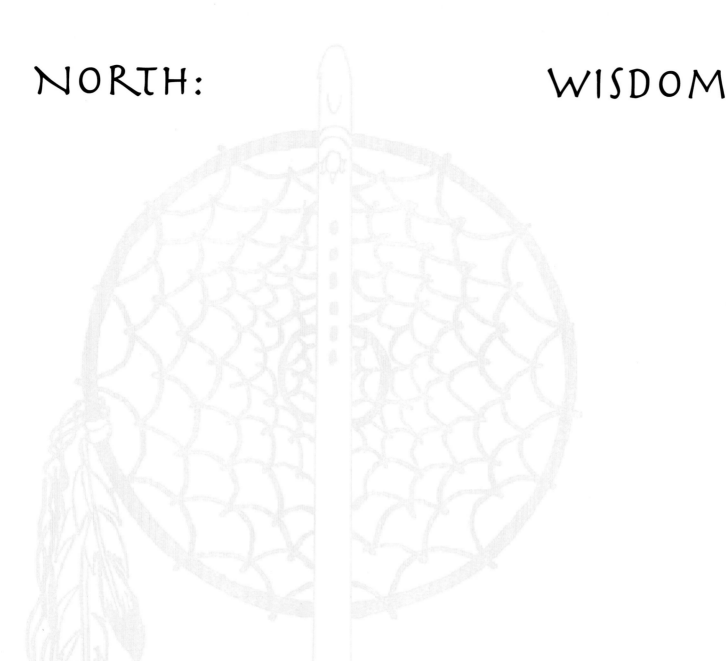

Spirit means, quite literally, breath. As we breathe in, we in-spire. We direct this spirit into the Flute to create a vibration, or tone. You are beginning to discover the pleasures of receiving the tone of the Flute into your body. That tone is resonating (which means re-sounding) in your muscles, bones, and organs, and back into the air, deeply enriched by the experience! As you begin to perceive the tone more deeply, allow your inner ear to conceive of the sound you desire. Let that inner vibration guide and direct your body to express the sound you seek, healing and harmonizing with your inner beauty.

In the light of your expanding awareness, repeat *Lesson 2* as often as you like. Journal your experiences on the Dreamcatcher, and when you are ready, journey on to *Lesson 3*.

LESSON 3:
THE TALKING FLUTE

You arrive at your rock at sunrise, eager for your next visit with the Master. Fragrant wildflowers nod their sleepy heads under the full fresh green canopy of late Spring leaves. While waiting, you weave a long luxuriant melody through the foliage. Where is the Master? Suddenly, a mockingbird alights on a branch, just a few feet from your face. He cocks his head to the side and lets out a short burst of song. How will you answer?

EAST: INITIATION

ARTICULATION

Go back to the Prelude and read it aloud without consonants: "-ou a--i-e a- -ou- -o- a- -u--i--, ea-e- -o- -ou- -e-- -i-i- -i- --e a-e." Doesn't make much sense! The Breath provides the "vowels" of the Flute; while the tongue provides the consonants. How we begin and end a note is called "articulation." Just as we shape words with a variety of consonants, we can shape tones with a variety of articulations.

Hold your palm 3 or 4 inches in front of your face. Blow a steady stream of air. Now repeat, initiating the stream with your tongue, as if to say "tu." Try several in a row: tu-tu-tu-tu. Experiment with more gentle and aggressive tonguing, and with different rhythms.

Now try the same with the Flute. Start with a series of tu's on a single note, then expand to other notes, and moving between notes. Again, experiment with more gentle and aggressive tu's.

Now play 2 or 3 notes in a row, but only initiate the first one with the tongue. Notes that are played in sequence without tonguing are called "slurred." Improvise, mixing up a variety of tongued and slurred notes. Enjoy the new interest, character, and expression available to you and your talking Flute.

DYNAMICS

"Dynamics" refers to the physical energy carried by the sound wave—the loudness or softness of our tone.

Choose a fingering and prepare to blow a single long note with your best playing position and tone. Begin by blowing as soft as possible—try to blow so softly that the sound merely whistles, groans, and scratches. These sounds may be put to wonderful use—see *Lesson 6*. Gradually increase the volume of air: you will reach a threshold at which the tone sounds consistent. That is the soft end of the dynamic range for that note.

Continue this exercise, gradually increasing the volume of air. The increasing dynamic volume is called "crescendo" (cre-SHEN-do), which means "growing" in Italian. As you grow your sound, you will reach another threshold where the sound seems to "break" into a higher pitched squawk. That is the loud end of the dynamic range for that note.

The dynamic range of Native American Flutes varies tremendously from Flute to Flute, depending on materials and construction. (See *Appendix*) The range can be enhanced by the exercises in *Lesson 2*: by bringing the sound inside and using our bodies to resonate, we can strengthen the consistency of the soft end and the resonance of the loud end.

Turn South to learn how to further shape your musical words with articulation and dynamics…

SOUTH: PRACTICE
ARTICULATION EXERCISES

We will use the musical symbol known as a quarter note

to stand for a single note played for one beat. (See *Lesson 4* for more explanation.) Choose any four notes on the Flute, and play them steadily in sequence, beginning each note with tu.

For example:

Written in quarter notes, what you just played looks like this:

When you put rhythm and notes together in Nakai TAB notation, they look like this:

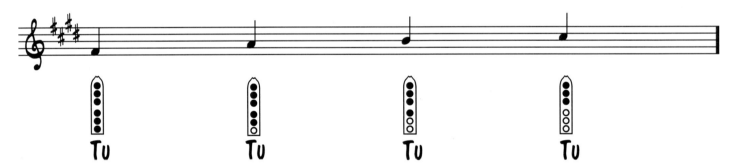

Now start the first note with tu and finger the other ones without tonguing (slur). In musical notation, this articulation looks like this:

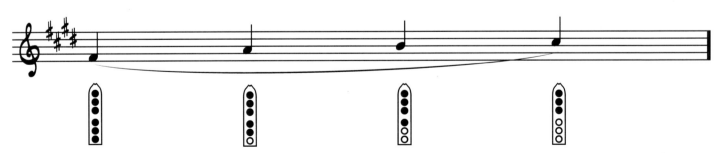

The curved line represents the slur—the note at the start of the curve is tongued, while the others are not.

WARNING!

The following exercises involve constructing new neural pathways in your brain. Mastering them will give you a tremendous amount of control and variety in your musical expression—yet even a small amount of attention will be enough to transform your playing. So, if at any point you feel your brain frying, I highly recommend that you take frequent breaks to freely improvise, exploring tongued and slurred notes.

Now, using the same four notes, try different combinations of slurred and tongued notes: **16**

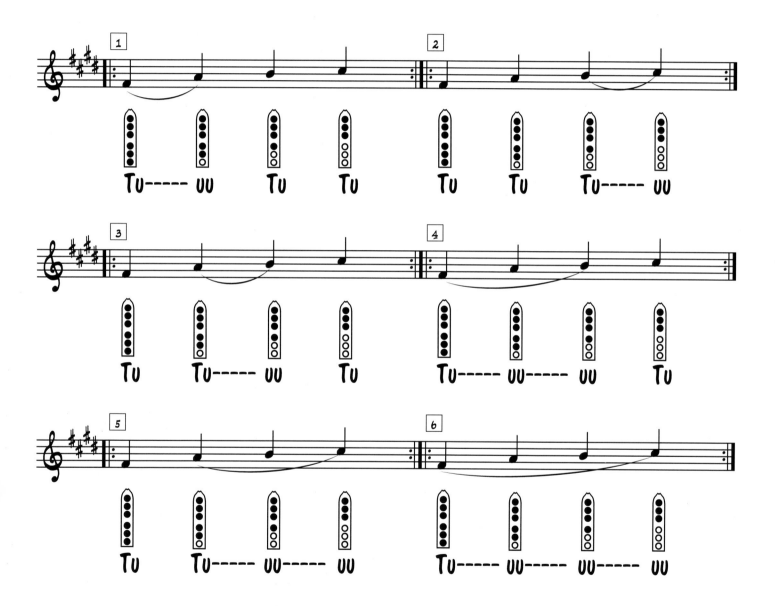

Repeat each pattern until mastered. Try with as many different sets of four fingerings as you want. (There are 1110 possible 4-note combinations in the Traditional Scale that do not repeat any notes in a row!)

Now try these trickier ones:

ARTICULATION KUNG-FU!!

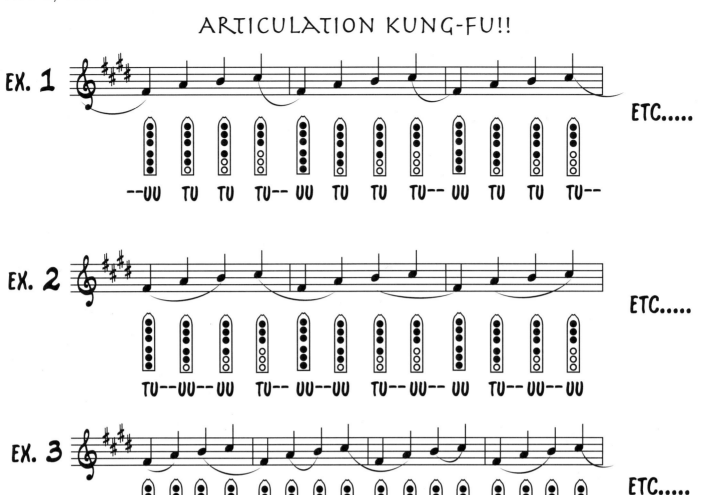

So far, all these patterns have been based on four-note groups. Create your own articulation patterns based on different groupings of notes—3's, 5's, 6's, 7's… Also, most students first choose four scale notes in sequence, ascending or descending. Try sequences of notes that skip around and/or change direction. That way, this exercise can open you up to infinite new melodic ideas, as well as articulation.

DYNAMICS EXERCISES

Play a long tone. Begin softly, and grow louder, then back to soft again. Repeat and listen carefully to the pitch. Does it get a little higher as you blow harder and lower as you blow softer? Rising or falling of pitch together with dynamics can be used with great artistry, or just sound out of tune. Explore and enjoy this phenomenon.

The amount of pitch fluctuation associated with dynamics varies widely from Flute to Flute. If you have access to more than one Flute, especially by different makers, try this exercise on them all. Some will blow freely, others will offer more resistance, or backpressure. These factors combine to produce different levels of pitch fluctuation and dynamics.

Blowing harder or softer is not the only factor in controlling dynamics and pitch. With a consistent level of breath support, sing "ooooooo-aaaaaaah." Which was louder? Sounds sound louder in a larger resonating chamber. We can use the same principles playing the Flute (See *Lesson 2*).

Repeat the crescendo-decrescendo exercise, opening and bringing the sound inside as you grow louder and softer. Experiment with levels of breath support from the diaphragm. You will find much greater control over the pitch fluctuation as well, as you connect more and more of your body and mind to the creation and enjoyment of your sound!

WEST: TRANSFORMATION

Articulation can vary as much as the consonants in the alphabet. A sharp "tu" accompanied by a burst of air (an aspirated "tu") can produce a short squeak or hiccupping sound. Experiment with a variety of tus from sharp and aspirated to subtle and gentle. Lus, dus, rus, and kus can all be quite effective. Languages other than English have more consonants to offer—try a gentle throat-clearing consonant as you might find in a French ru or in German, Hebrew, or Arabic. Roll your rus as in Spanish or Italian—this is known as "flutter-tongue." Each one of these as many variations: for example, you can extend the roll through the note, or initiate a note with a few flaps of the tongue.

Dynamics can be used in broad sweeps or in subtle, rapidly changing shapes—what I call "micro-dynamics." The Talking Flute combines articulation and dynamics in myriad ways to shape each note. Flutemaker Odell Borg demonstrates this beautifully and simply in his YouTube videos—what he calls, "Singing with the Breath." Here's a graphic representation of the dynamics of the sound waves produced by equal articulation and dynamics.

Now feast your eyes on the Talking Flute: ⬥18

THE KLEZMER AND THE TALKING FLUTE

For 15 years I devoted my musical life to playing the traditional Jewish instrumental music of Eastern Europe on the silver flute. A musician in this style is a klezmer, which derives from Hebrew words meaning "vessel of song." When I first began, few contemporary flutists had attempted this style, leaving me with very expressive clarinetists and violinists for inspiration.

In traditional Jewish culture, everything is sung—daily prayer, sacred service, even schooling. Thus the instrumental music interweaves closely with the spoken language. Klezmer circles give much attention to characteristic ornaments (see *Lesson 6*-West), but I found that these were not enough to give my playing a hearty "yiddishe tam" (Jewish flavor).

That is when I began to extensively develop a much wider range of articulation combined with micro-dynamics—the Talking Flute. When I returned to classical, jazz, and other forms of music—eventually turning to the Native American Flute—the Talking Flute breathed vivid life into everything I played.

NORTH: WISDOM

A mockingbird is only so patient. He cocks his head, regarding you quizzically, thinking, "What planet did this creature drop from? Fluto? Perhaps it requires more explanation." The bird launches into a burst of hodgepodge melodies, trying every song he knows on you. You boldly answer with your Talking Flute, and launch into a lively conversation…

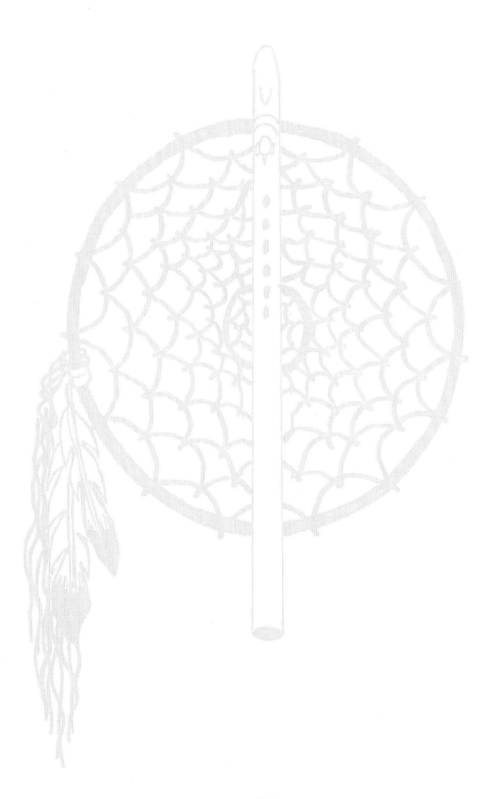

LESSON 4: TIME

As dawn passes to morning, the first crickets blend their song with the sweet trill of the meadowlarks. A surge of warmth from the rising sun heralds the heat to come. As you converse with birdsong and breezes, you feel the roll of the Earth and her flight round the Sun.

Music is an art of time. We measure the very pitches themselves by how many times they vibrate in a second. Melodies evolve through shifting patterns of sounds and silences of various durations. Through music, the stubbornly ticking seconds become infinitely flexible clay for our play and creation of exquisite structures.

EAST: INITIATION

20

Set up some sort of recording device (a cell phone can easily accompany you to your rock), pick up your Flute and play. Listen back to yourself, attentive to the patterns of sound and silence. Did you play a stream of notes of roughly equal value? Did you vary the length of the notes, long and short? Did you create a repeating pattern, for example short short long, short short long? Did you play slow? Fast? Changing speeds? Did you include silent pauses at regular or irregular intervals?

Rhythm is the durations of the sounds and silences in music, and the relationship between those durations. Western music measures these durations against an implied steady pulse, known as beat. This progression of beats can be seen as a ruler. A note can last one beat or more—

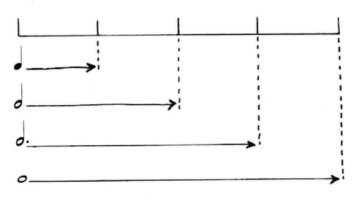

or less

Western music notates the silences equal to these durations as well.
Return to your Flute. Experiment with playing longer and shorter notes. Record and listen.

VALUE OF SOUND "NOTE"	=	VALUE OF SILENCE "REST"
♪		𝄾
♪		𝄾
♩		𝄽
♩		–
𝅝		–

28

The beat "ruler" governs the relationship between the lengths of the notes, but unlike a yardstick, the length of the beat itself varies widely, as implied pulse goes faster and slower. Similar to our own hearts, the regular pulse will run at different rates. Western music calls this phenomenon *tempo* (plural: *tempi*).

To get a feeling for tempo, tap your foot to a steady beat and play along. Once you have a good flow going, speed up the tapping of your foot, keeping your Flute "locked in" to the foot taps. Now try a slower tempo. Experiment with accelerating and decelerating foot taps.

STEALING TIME

In much of popular music, the tempo is absolutely steady from beginning to end. In Western Classical music, we often hear the tempo slow down and speed up. There is another treatment of tempo found in Classical music, particularly suited to our Native American Flute, in which the music slows or speeds up more freely to fully express the shape of the melody. Since this style of playing lives outside the box of steady tempo, the Italians called it "rubato"—"stolen" time.

Now combine your tempo exercise with your rhythm exercise, varying the lengths of the sounds and silences within the different tempi. Play freely with these concepts until you are ready for more disciplined exercises that await you in the South.

SOUTH: PRACTICE

While our flowing Fluting to this point may have seemed very free and unstructured, with careful and honest listening to ourselves we discover that we've been imposing all kinds of habits, patterns, unwritten rules, and limits—mostly unconsciously. With greater conscious awareness and mastery of structure we become more free!

Choose and play three notes. Now play them each as long as possible, now each as short as possible. Introduce silences between them—vary the length of the silences and the notes. Now add the various articulations and tone color variations from the previous Lessons. Play them over and over one way; then switch to another. Change the order of the notes.

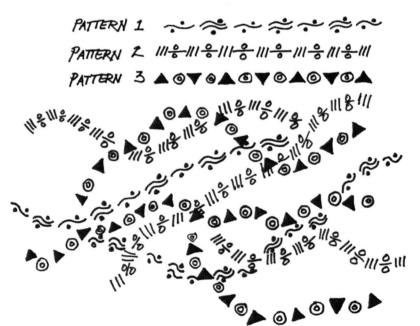

Repetition and variation form the structures of music in time. I have often described music as the interplay between expectations and surprises: repetition sets up the expectations and variation contributes the surprises. The surprises do not exist without the expectations. Thus, an improvisation with constant variation can become quite tedious—the variation becomes the expectation. The restless player tires quickly. Relax your mind and enjoy the subtle nuances. Repetition can give great meaning to the subtlest variation.

Now choose from one of the rhythmic patterns you created with your 3 notes. Repeat this pattern, but change the notes—each time, or once in

You may experiment with other elements from the Lessons, keeping one constant and varying the others. (See *Lesson 5*-East for a synopsis of these elements.)

Limiting resources immensely stimulates our creativity! Ludwig van Beethoven built his entire Fifth Symphony around one four-note rhythmic idea: short-short-short-long.

String together your three-note ideas. A short musical idea is called a "motive." Notes are like letters, motives like words, motives strung together form phrases—musical sentences. Phrases together form musical stories.

The most difficult part of playing the Native American Flute is to know when to stop! All stories consist of a beginning, middle, and end. Let your stories end, leaving enough silence to relax and digest the musical meal you have just so generously served. Play freely and observe how your previous meanderings have been transformed into purposeful journeys!

WEST: TRANSFORMATION

The following exercise, which is inspired by W. A. Mathieu's wonderful **The Listening Book** (© 1991, Shambhala, Boston), provides a fertile field in which to seed the ideas discussed in this lesson. Bring a clock with a second hand, or a friend with a stopwatch (you might have one on your cell phone) to your rock. Without looking at the clock, attempt to play a short improvisation for exactly 10 seconds. Look at the clock when you are finished and check your accuracy. Practice this discipline until you get pretty close every time; then practice it some more!

The 10-second improvisation exercise is like eating just one chocolate out of the whole box.

CLOCKOLATES

At first, longing to eat more chocolates may overcome our experience of the one we're eating—we wonder, "Did I choose the best one?" Then we learn to savor the luscious morsel, discovering a symphony of flavors and fragrance tucked away in the tiny package. Even after the candy has melted away in our mouths, we savor the subtle aftertastes and mouthwatering memories. This experience exponentially enriches our pleasure the next time we open the box.

Experiment with other time-limited improvisations: 5, 12, 20, 40, and 60 seconds all work well. Soon you will find yourself creating one exquisite musical truffle after another!

NORTH: WISDOM

All creation expresses in rhythm—from the rapid oscillation of the hummingbird's wings to the slowly shifting seasons. As we create music, we more fully perceive, experience, and master time. Continue exploring the exercises within this lesson, and journal your insights and experiences.

LESSON 5: THE CENTER

Layer upon layer of twittering, scratching, and chugging insect rhythms assault your ears as you lie, eyes wide open beneath the open window, hoping to catch a cooling breeze. Unable to sleep, you head for the rock, Flute in hand. Flashing fireflies and the bright moon light your way—though not enough to warn when the occasional moth or whirring beetle collides with your head. You reach the rock; sit down to play. At first the Flutesong feels lost in the din. You sway gently with the incessant rhythms, then rise up and dance. You raise the Flute again to your lips, mimic the katydid with one long note. More dance is followed by another single note, until, one note at a time, your dancing Flutesong sails and weaves with the music of the summer night.

"GOD IS A SPHERE WHOSE CENTER IS EVERYWHERE, CIRCUMFERENCE IS NOWHERE"—EMPEDOCLES

EAST: INITIATION

We perceive time by what changes and what stays the same. I call the part that stays the same "The Center." In music, we can choose different musical elements, or combinations of elements, to be that center. In *Lesson 4* we used rhythmic motives; in *Lesson 5* we will use pitches.

Let's begin by exploring the different pitches from which we will choose our center. For now we will limit ourselves to the notes of the traditional scale. Choose one note. Just one note! Close your eyes, and blow several long tones on that note—till the end of your breath. Listen to that note, enjoy it, get to know its character.

Now expand your improvisation on this note, using all the musical ideas we have explored so far. These ideas can be categorized under the four basic characteristics of a musical tone, which I refer to as **FAT-D**:

1. **Frequency:** the speed of vibration, producing the pitch (highness and lowness). In our one-note improvisation, the fundamental pitch will remain constant—although it may vary slightly with tools such as vibrato (*Lesson 2*).
2. **Amplitude:** the amount of energy carried by the sound wave (loudness and softness). See *Lesson 3* on Dynamics.
3. **Timbre** (pronounced TAM-ber), a.k.a. Tone Color: the quality, or character of the tone. In Native American Flute circles, this is referred to as the "voice" of the Flute. We experimented with varied tone colors in our Flutonian exercises (*Lesson 2*).
4. **Duration:** the length of the tone. Rhythm refers to the patterns of durations of sounds and silences. Since we are limited to one pitch, rhythm will be the element of melody used to structure our one-note stories.

Add to these the elements of articulation (*Lesson 3*) and structures in time (*Lesson 4*). Use these ideas and concepts in your play as you tell a whole musical story on a single note.

Repeat this exercise for each note of the traditional scale; or, if you wish, continue South and bounce back East when you are ready to initiate a new center.

Now that you have established your expression with each of the six pitches of the traditional scale, move South to re-center…

SOUTH: PRACTICE

Play several short free improvisations. For each, note what note you start on and what note you end on and jot down the fingerings. Many beginning Flutists start and end their improvisations on the lowest note of the Flute, all six holes covered—though you may have branched out from this tendency by now. Western music calls the ending tone the "tonic." The tone we choose to end on becomes our "home base"—the Center to which all the other pitches are relating somehow. The choice of tonic sets up the pattern of tonal relationships that are known as a mode.

SCALE OR MODE?

I like to look at a scale as a simple abstract set of pitches, arranged from low to high. A mode, then, is a scale with an attitude. In the simple sense, we will be changing the center, or tonic, to a pitch other than the lowest note, producing a different pattern of tonal relationships. The modes produced by this method can be said to be the modes of the traditional scale, since they all share the same set of pitches. In many cultures, modes can include melodic motives, different notes going down than up, and even extramusical associations (morning modes, summer modes, happy or sad modes...)

We will now experiment with establishing different centers, and thus different modes, using the different notes of the traditional scale as tonics. The most fun way to do this is to find a friend with a Flute in the same key as yours (see textbox).

KEY IDEAS

The "key" of the Native American Flute is customarily considered the Western pitch that correlates with the tonic of the pentatonic minor scale, which begins on its lowest note. Flutes are labeled and sold according to key, and the letter name is usually carved on the underside of the Flute.

You can do this exercise with other instruments as well, as long as you've figured out the same scale on both instruments. In absence of a conspirator ("conspire" = "breathe together"), you may record your own drone on the Flute or another instrument and jam along with the playback.

MODES AND DRONES

One friend will drone on a single note while the other will improvise with the notes of the traditional scale, then switch.

Begin with the lowest note in the scale as the drone (the center, the tonic).

Relax into the mode, then jot down a few words, draw a picture or mix a color regarding its mood below:

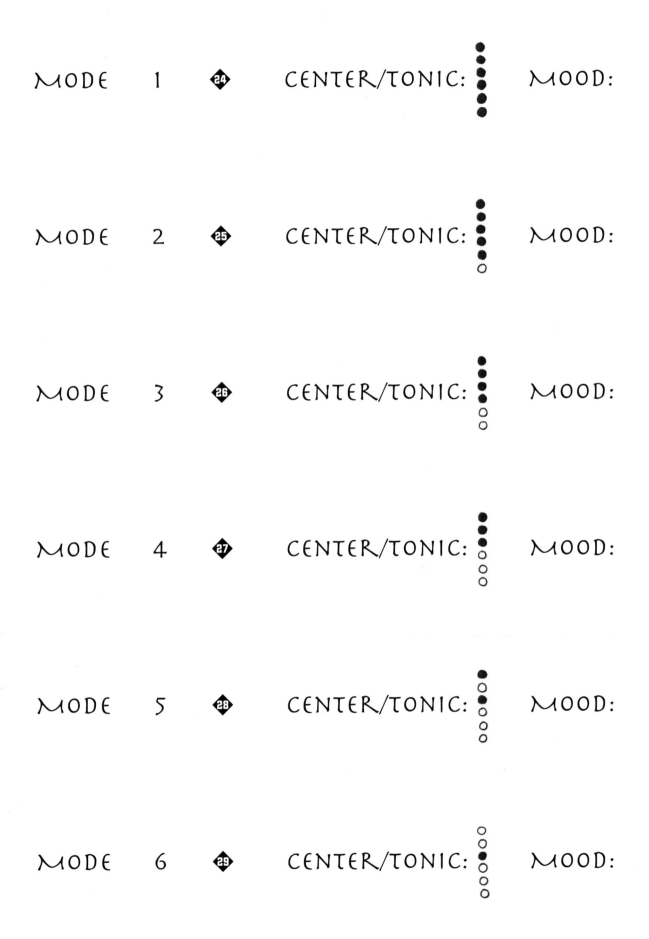

MODE 1 ◈ 24 CENTER/TONIC: MOOD:

MODE 2 ◈ 25 CENTER/TONIC: MOOD:

MODE 3 ◈ 26 CENTER/TONIC: MOOD:

MODE 4 ◈ 27 CENTER/TONIC: MOOD:

MODE 5 ◈ 28 CENTER/TONIC: MOOD:

MODE 6 ◈ 29 CENTER/TONIC: MOOD:

THE 6 MODES OF THE TRADITIONAL SCALE IN NAKAI TAB:

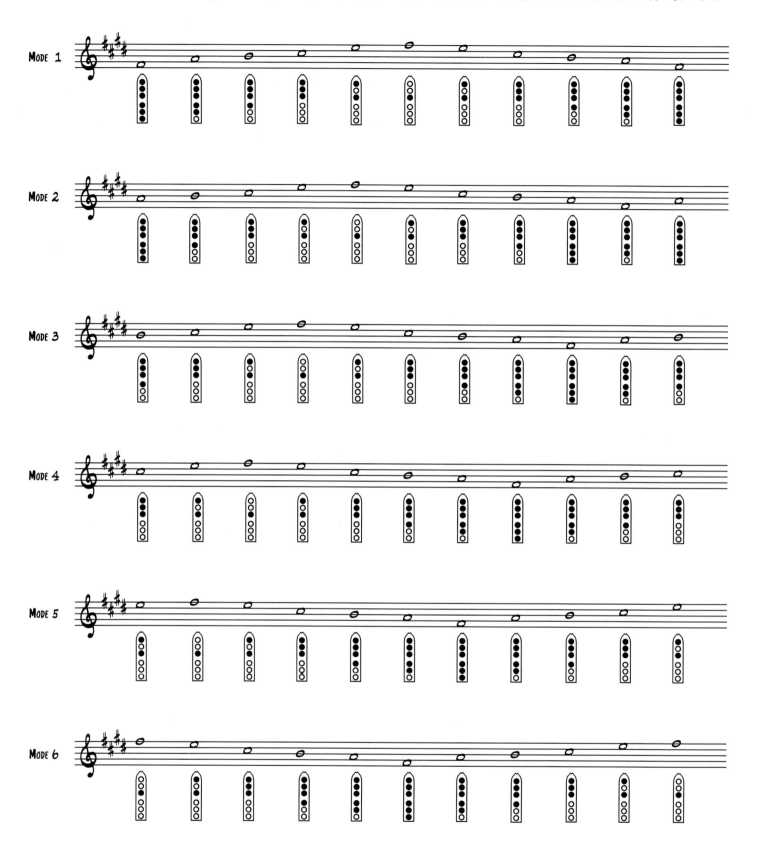

Note that the improviser will use the same set of notes regardless of the drone, yet through the remarkable chemistry of tonal gravity, the improvisation will completely change character depending on the drone note. Different modes may inspire different styles of playing—an energetic mode may want to express with fast, staccato notes; a noble mode with stately long tones. Listen and play with these tendencies.

36

OCTAVES

In Western musical terms, these two notes

carry the same name—the higher note vibrates twice as fast as the lower. This interval known as an "octave"—since they are eight notes apart in the Western scale system. Most musical cultures recognize this phenomenon, but not all assign the same meaning or character to the notes in different octaves. While Modes 1 and 6 are technically the same in Western musical terms, I find their character to be substantially different on the Native American Flute. What have you discovered?

To learn how to make this awareness a deep aspect of your Flutesong without adopting your own personal droner, go West!

WEST: TRANSFORMATION

OUT AND BACK

Pick a center note (tonic) from one of the modes you discovered in the South. Play a long tone, then evolve into a one note improvisation. Gradually add one or two new notes at a time, returning frequently to your center. Venture further out, with longer phrases of melody in between your returns to center, then spiral back home.

You will find that the melody expresses with the mood and characteristics that you wrote down for the mode you have chosen. Repeat the exercise on each mode. Without learning any new notes, your range of melodic expression has increased exponentially!

"Out and Back" spirals into a sublime structure that brings an overarching sense of compositional unity to even the longest improvisations. Now create a small 3 or 4 note motive to use as your center (see *Lesson 4: South*), and repeat the exercise…

MOVABLE DRONES

Repeat Modes and Drones and/or Out and Back, moving the center every once and a while. This is known as a harmonic progression. Many harmonic progressions eventually return to the first tonic, but yours doesn't have to…explore

NORTH: WISDOM

After your dance and song at the rock, the summer night finally makes sense. Return to your rest; close your eyes. In your dream, you find yourself in a village that vibrates to a Flute tone. One day, after you have become warm, comfortable, and friendly with the villagers, you find a small stone in your pocket. You rub it, and find yourself in a new village, vibrating to a new tone. You repeat the friendship process, and similarly travel to the next village.

Once you have befriended all six villages, you rub your stone and find yourself flying high above them all. You can easily see the lay of the land and the many pathways; and even the relationships, creativity, and love that weave between the harmonious inhabitants of the Land of Six Villages.

Journal your dreams and experiences.

LESSON 6:
ADDING TO THE WHOLE—
THERE ARE NO WRONG NOTES!

A sudden burst of birdsong rouses you in the early morning. As you turn to your window, the green dreams of early spring rattle against the red autumn leaves that fill your opening eyes. Stepping outside, boisterous legions of feasting flocks celebrate the journey south. Chattering squirrels dash about gathering acorns as the bluebirds and yellow-breasted meadowlarks flit from the red leaves to the still-green grass. Undulating V's of geese overhead echo noble honks. Hoping for some calm, you breath into your Flute. The first squawk surprises you, but soon you find your fingers dancing over the holes, mimicking the twitters, chatters, and honks; celebrating like a kid at a birthday party.

Our holes fully covered, our tone round and full, we have explored in depth the six tones. Yet the inadvertent squawks we worked so hard to eliminate in *Lesson 1* hint that other Flute sounds may be available to us. All these sounds can be made into music, if we choose. There are no wrong notes!

EAST: INITIATION

ONE LITTLE, TWO LITTLE, THREE LITTLE NEW NOTES

Such wonders we have discovered with only six notes! And I tell you there are treasures that lie beyond! Let us add one note:

Do some Flutonian long tones and some 1-note improvisations to become friendly with the sound of this note. Notice that we finally raise our left hand ring finger. This will take some getting used to. Practice alternating this fingering with all the others that you know so far, like this:

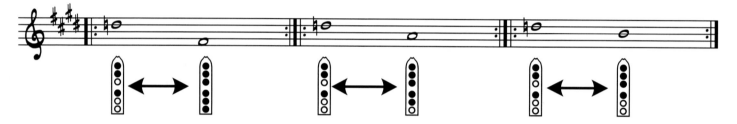

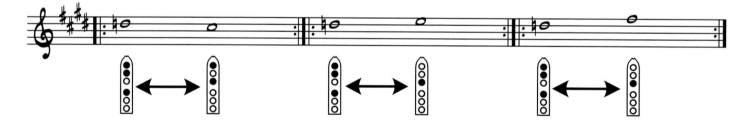

Now let's add a high note. When playing this note, you may give a more oomph to your breath support to hear it speak in its high register. This note may speak better on different Flutes with different fingerings. (You may want to consult with your Flutemaker—many Flutes come with a fingering chart, and some makers post their fingerings online.) See which one sounds best to you.

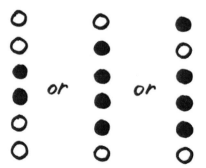

Repeat the long tones, one-note improvisation, and alternating fingerings (this time including our other new note) to master this note.

Once you can easily play this note in its high register, add this note,

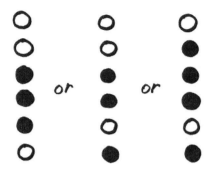

repeating the same process of exploration.

THE WESTERN MAJOR SCALE

These three notes open up the world of the Western Major Scale—the familiar do-re-mi-fa-so-la-ti-do—to Native American Flute players. Here is the fingering for that scale—

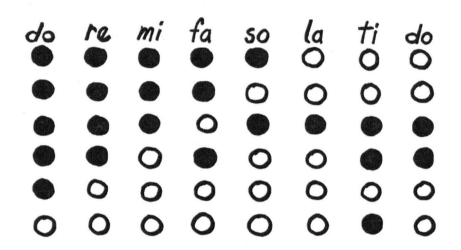

—and the Nakai TAB

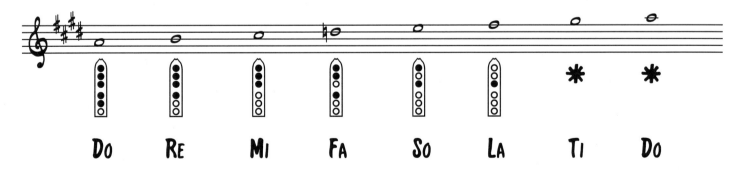

*Note that the fingerings for Ti and high Do vary widely from flute to flute. Consult your Flutemaker's fingering charts, or experiment with the fingerings provided above.

Many familiar songs will fall neatly under your fingers as you become more fluent in this scale. Great satisfaction awaits as you apply the exercises of *Lesson 5* to discover a whole new set of modes. But we haven't made it this far without a passion for adventure! Before slipping into the comforts of the common culture, let us breathe with nature to unlock the mysteries that lie under our fingers!

SOUTH: PRACTICE

BREATHING INTO NEW TERRITORY

Let us revisit our third little new note. Instead of reaching for the higher tone, blow very gently to produce a lower tone. The same fingering produces two different notes, one high and clear, another low and delicate. Now under-blow even more, until the tone becomes a chattering of groans and whistles. Changing registers by over-blowing or under-blowing is one way to discover new sounds in the Flute. When we stop trying to make every tone as full, round, and loud as possible we open up the door to limitless new grunts, squeals, whistles—such as we may hear in nature.

The fingering on the right is one of my favorites.

On my Flutes, with a little shift in breath support the note slips easily from the higher to lower pitch, imitating the call of the crane.

34

MAPPING YOUR EXPLORATIONS

Here are all the possible full-hole fingerings on the Native American Flute:

Before you get out your magnifying glass, have fun figuring these out and drawing them for yourself. You may wish to explore these new fingerings here and there, or take a more systematic approach, covering each and every possible fingering in a chosen order. I structure my students' explorations into the wilds of new Flute sounds with a Flute Journal—the Flutist's version of a naturalist's notebook. Observe the sample page on the right.

The very technically minded may even wish to employ an electric tuner to measure the precise pitches of their discoveries.

A NOTE ON THE FLUTE JOURNAL:

Thoroughly exploring every one of the 64 multi-toned fingerings is no small task—and may prove to be quite unnecessary. As we have experienced, much music can be made with a few notes. Always remember to keep it fun! Try a few, move on, try something else, come back to it—let your intuition guide you as to when and how much of this exercise you practice.

6/13/2011

Fingering:

blue flower

Color: medium blue

Emotion: lonely call

Similar to: , but tone is more clear

Overblows: with effort, produces a high piercing pitch with a "shadow" airy pitch underneath

Bends easily with changing breath pressure

Meditation: Campfire scene in autumn – the story teller begins an epic tale...

SETTING UP CAMP

Now that we have all these new sounds, what can we do with them? How do we integrate them into what we have already learned with our scales and modes? Hearing me improvise, a friend in the Alaska Flute Circle pronounced that I played with sounds rather than notes. You may choose to improvise entirely "out in the woods," alternate sections of modal improvisation with walks on the wild side, or spice up your traditional playing with an occasional bird call.

"ALTERNATE" FINGERINGS

Many Native American Flute fingering charts offer "alternate" fingerings for certain notes, that may sound better on different Flutes. While in your explorations you may discover notes of quite similar pitches, I encourage you to sensitize yourself to the slight variations in tone color, pitch and "behavior" of each fingering.

My best advice: let Nature be your guide! Listen to how she creates harmony from wind, water, and the myriad voices of her creatures. If you find your rock in the bedroom of a city apartment, hear the harmony in the rumble of traffic and the voices of children playing. See *Lesson 7* for more…

We can borrow from our previous exercises to integrate new fingerings and sounds into our musical vocabulary. Choose one fingering, and do a one-fingering improvisation. Note that now this fingering includes several notes and sounds. Then add another, and another. Usually three fingerings, with all their over- and under-blowing possibilities, are enough to keep you busy! You may add pages to your Flute Journal about these one, two, and three fingering improvisations.

Eventually, you may create your own scales and modes, selecting your own special tonal flowers from the vast and varied garden we have discovered.

From 6 tones to 64 multi-toned fingerings! What more could there be? Your Flute has more surprises in store as you head West…

WEST: TRANSFORMATION

MORE AND MORE AND MORE AND MORE...

So far, our map has included only full-hole fingerings. But *Lesson 1 's* squawks revealed that partial hole coverage can have certain...effects. Experiment with fingerings that partially cover one or more of the covered holes. Try ½ holes, ¼ holes, ¾ holes...suddenly our fingering possibilities expand from 64 to 3074 and more! Multiply that by the varied notes produced by under- and over-blowing and WAIT! STOP! This is getting WAY out of hand! Doesn't this guy have a life?

OK, alright, I confess. I have a life, a bride and three kids, several jobs, a music ministry, a house under construction, and no immediate plans to spend several years in a monastery journaling to master 3074 Flute fingerings.

SLIP-SLIDING AWAY

But I still love slipping and sliding my fingers on the holes of my Native American Flute. Play with sliding your fingers between the notes of the traditional scale. Sliding off is easier, and sliding on trickier, but very effective. With practice, you can produce a continuous smear from low to high and down again.

Sliding off middle fingerings (see illustration on the left) can produce very interesting effects.

Partial hole coverage can be used to bring a note more in "tune" or produce new notes and effects.

SPICY!

Homesick? Let us return to our trusty traditional scale and her mouthwatering modes. Improvise in the traditional scale, ending with a long tone on the lowest note. When you are ready to end the note, lift a bunch of fingers, push a little with the breath, and cut off the higher note with your tongue almost before it begins. Many Native American Flute players end their songs with this ornament, which I call a "yelp." Practice and experimentation with some of the fun fingerings discovered earlier in this lesson will produce a large variety of yelps. Experiment with yelps at different points in your improvisation, as well as reverse yelps (starting from the higher tone and landing on the lower tone).

Most world Flute players love to spice up their music with ornaments.

Ornaments combine fingers, breath, and articulation to alter the beginning, end, or middle of a note. Other ornaments and special effects include:

- Grace notes: One or several notes played very rapidly before a main note, or between two main notes in your melody (similar to reverse yelps, but often the grace notes are closer in pitch to the main tone).
- Finger Slides (see above) into, off of, or between notes. The breath can also be used to raise or lower the pitch ornamentally (see *Lesson 2*).
- Trills and Tremolos: rapid alternation of two notes. Trills are between adjacent tones in a scale, tremolos skip over one or more notes.

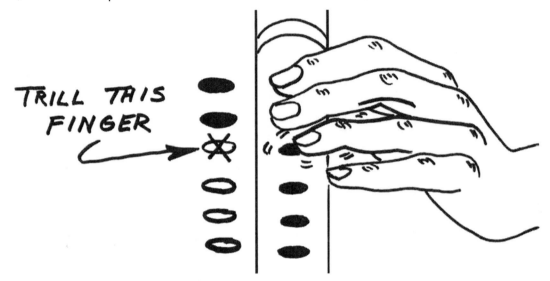

- Finger Vibrato: (AKA microtonal trill) rapidly shaking a finger over an uncovered hole or partial hole.
- Flutter tongue: rolling the tongue as one would the letter "r" in Italian. This can be done gently or forcefully; at the beginning of a note, all through, or at the end—for a great variety of effects. The rapid-fire bursts of air may even sound at different registers, creating a rich multiphonic explosion of sound.
- Finger Brushes: brush your fingers rapidly back and forth over the holes. One of the most fun ways is to cover holes 4, 5, 6 and brush the top three fingers over holes 1, 2, 3.

Now return to the traditional scale or another of your favorite modes. Improvise a breath of melody, experimenting with one or two ornaments and effects. With practice, you will begin to feel the ornament flow out of the melody, as naturally as a flower on a branch.

NORTH: WISDOM

Fluting joyfully on your rock, your song easily slips between the rattles and sighs of nature and the ancient melody that you are creating anew in this moment. Eyes closed, your mind journeys again to the vision of the Six Villages. With the eye of the eagle, you find yourself able to focus at will—not only on the villages and the pathways between them—but on every rock, flower, leaf, blade of grass, bird, bug, beast, and fish in every garden, meadow, woodland, stream and lake that lies between them. You select the images that move your own melody of tones and sounds, and your song becomes one movement in the harmony of the whole.

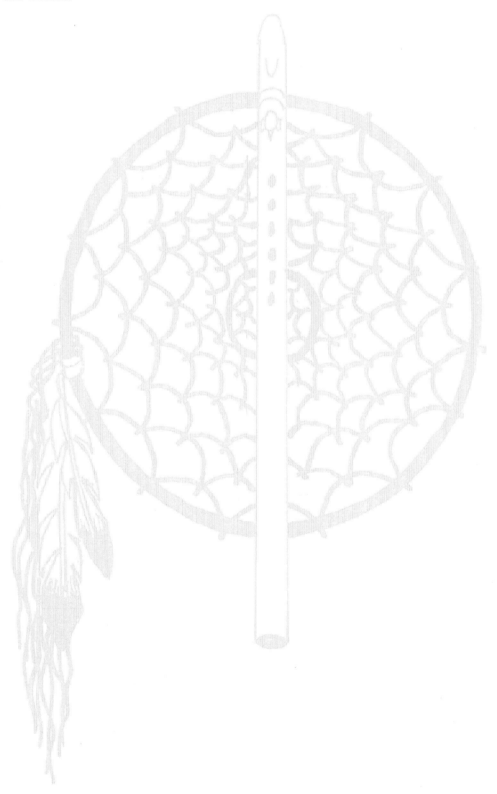

LESSON 7: SILENCE

A determined swoosh—crunch—swoosh—crunch rhythm accompanies your brisk walk through the fallen leaves. Browns and golds show forth against the crisp blue sky as the joyful crunching consumes the thoughts of the day. You reach the rock, and the crunching stops suddenly, stunned by complete silence. Your silent mind opens to receive the silence, interspersed with the gentle rattle of the occasional breeze in the dry oaks. After quite some time, you look down at the Flute in your hands, realizing that you haven't yet played a note.

*   *   *

HOW TO USE THIS LESSON

Our journey to Flute Mastery now crosses into new territories. Do not fear: you are well prepared. Along with your breathing, fingering, and articulation techniques you have developed your inner skills of perception and imagination. These inner skills now step to the foreground as we experience the Silence. Imagination is not "just pretend"—it is a tool of perception and creation. You can use the images in these lessons as a jumping off point for your own. Trust what you hear and see along your path, and then make music!

EAST: INITIATION

RAISE THE FLUTE TO YOUR LIPS. WAIT. LISTEN.

BEGIN TO PLAY A SINGLE BREATH OF MELODY. STOP. BREATHE. LISTEN.

Thus far, we have focused all our attention on sounds, which comprise only one half of music: Silence forms the other half. Too often our love of the Flute tone tempts us to produce a continuous stream of uninterrupted melody—we hardly want to stop to catch our breath. In this lesson we will learn more about the Silence and how to embrace it.

Once upon a time, the prophet Elijah stood on upon a rock…

And he said, Go forth, and stand upon the mount before the LORD. And, behold, the LORD passed by, and a great and strong wind rent the mountains, and brake in pieces the rocks before the LORD; but the LORD was not in the wind: and after the wind an earthquake; but the LORD was not in the earthquake: And after the earthquake a fire; but the LORD was not in the fire: and after the fire a still small voice. (1 Kings 19: 11-12)

LORD OF THE FLUTE

In the English Bible, LORD stands for the Hebrew YHVH יהוה (Read Hebrew letters right to left). Here is one possible explanation of the Hebrew letters:

- Yod י, the hand, joins with

- Hay ה, the breath, (in-*Hay*-le, ex-*Hay*-le)

- to Vav ו, the vertical line, or ray of light connecting inner and outer (the Flute!)

- resulting again in breath ה.

SOUTH: PRACTICE

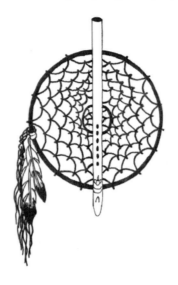

SILENCE AND BREATH:

Inhale.

Exhale a breath's-worth of melodious Flute tones. At the end of the breath, relax.

Receive the gift of a luxurious inhale.

Listen. When you are ready, form your exhalation into another beautiful breath's-worth of melody.

Breath brings a natural understanding of Silence. We compose each breath in two movements, Inbreath and Outbreath. Our present culture fears the silence of the Inbreath—the very source of Life—calling silence "dead air." We rush about trying to fill the dead air with busy noise. Haven't we learned that to In-spire is to live, and to Ex-spire is to die? Practice improvising in the rhythm of slow, steady breath; enjoying the Inbreath to receive life, quiet the mind, and to listen.

SILENCE IN THE CENTER

In *Lesson 4* we placed a rhythm in the center; *Lesson 5* a tonic pitch and then a motive. Here let us place Silence in the center of our musical creation. Practice "Out and Back" (*Lesson 5*: West) always returning to Silence as the central motive. Be patient and trusting as your fear of dead air drops away…

BREATHING WITH NATURE

Silence is rarely soundless. Whether the whirr of the computer fan, or the chirr of the cricket—many voices sing in the silence of our Inbreath. Listen and welcome these sounds into your music.

WEST: TRANSFORMATION

SHAPING THE SILENCE

Inbreath and Outbreath flow in a natural dialogue of sound and silence, each molding and shaping the other. Shape your improvisations with longer and shorter breaths. Add silence in small places, placing pauses of different lengths within the contour of longer phrases. Try longer silences, several long breaths of listening deeply, followed by a single long note or a joyful birdsong burst. Sound and Silence dance together—the bride and groom in their first dance and the lifelong companions dancing at their Golden Anniversary.

NATURE IN THE CENTER

Nature sounds make a beautiful background for the woody tones of the Native American Flute. Take this a step farther: allow the sounds of Nature to become an equal partner in making music.

Repeat "Breathing with Nature," placing Nature at the Center of your improvisation. Listen lovingly, and respond in kind. As your are listening to the conversation, imagine yourself standing on the next hill, listening to the distant Flute song weaving in and out of the breezes as naturally as the birds.

Now stop and listen more. Open the sphere of your awareness farther, hearing the harmony of all the sounds and silences around you. With practice and faith, you will begin to perceive the Center. There is melody in this center. Breathe it in, raise your flute to your lips, and allow this melody to move through you into the Flute.

Once you have discovered this melody, practice "Out and Back," traveling and exploring the sphere of sounds and silences within your perception.

NORTH: WISDOM

LISTEN...

LESSON 8:
THE HEART

The silent oaks surround you, bare branches scratching at the grey light of early dawn. The song of the Master rings again through the cold air of your dream. Suddenly awake—he must be at the rock this morning. Down the well-worn path, break into a run. Your anticipation shape-shifts to joy, dancing to the rhythm of your feet drumming the earth. You arrive at the rock, raise your Flute to your lips, calling fervently to the Master in song. The drumming continues, the drumming of your beating heart. Your song dances through the oaks to the cold winter sky.

EAST: INITIATION

Frequently heard in Native American Flute Circles: "Play from the Heart, not the Head." We often talk about the heart, but just what do we mean by it? So far, our lessons have contained plenty to keep our heads busy, in order to establish a vocabulary for the heart to express. Let us now turn to the heart itself, and discover how to open our music to its secrets.

There is much confusion about the heart: some say follow the head, not the heart—that following the heart leads to emotional chaos—while others say follow the heart, not the head—that following the head alone leads to coldness and cruelty. A wise teacher once counseled me to live from my heart, but not my emotions: the heart and the emotions are not the same thing. So how can we tangibly differentiate and feel our hearts and play our music from the heart?

WHAT IS THE HEART?

The heart is a powerful muscle that circulates blood to every corner of the body. The blood carries the breath (oxygen) and nutrients to every cell, and carries waste to the liver, kidneys, and lungs to be eliminated from the body. Thus the heart is vital (life-giving) to, and in touch with, all of our physical being. It resembles a fresh spring that pumps out water to nourish and replenish the earth.

Yet throughout time we have experienced feelings, desires, and messages in this muscle, though modern common sense would place these functions in the brain. A mysterious bundle of nerves lies in the center of the heart. Science hasn't really figured what it is doing there, but you can. Sit or stand tall. Breathe deep, and open your arms as if to receive an embrace...

SOUTH: PRACTICE

Stay open, and raise the Flute to your lips. You will find yourself in the balanced, open playing position described in *Lesson 1*. Note that if you keep your arms (and heart!) open, the Flute will tend to rise up, rather than point down.

Breathe, and use your mind to direct the breath to the heart. Now breathe the heart's breath into the Flute.

As the breath activates the tone, receive the tone inside the body, this time moving beyond the throat into the heart. This completes the cycle, circulating sound as the physical heart circulates the blood in the body.

What did you experience? Write it down if you desire. You experienced nothing? Don't let that stop you! Keep practicing and listening, and you will develop the awareness of the heart and its expression in your music. What at first may feel strange and vulnerable will become a familiar and pleasurable bubbling mixture of physical, emotional, mental and spiritual sensations flowing into your Flute song and touching the hearts of all who desire to hear.

WEST: TRANSFORMATION

Physiologically, our lungs are doing the breathing, but we can use the breath to bring awareness to all parts of our body, our Flutes, and beyond—and, through the circulating heart and the movement created by the lungs and diaphragm, the breath touches our whole body in a very direct way. The practices outlined in these lessons have led to greater awareness of the functioning of our minds and bodies as we fulfill the desire to create with music.

When we open ourselves to the expression of our hearts, we place ourselves upon the line, without armor, without pretense. I have yet to meet anyone who has not experienced life transformations following the choice to play the Flute. You have chosen the Native American Flute, an Instrument of the Heart for thousands of years, which finds the strength of the warrior in the heart of the maiden, the thunder in the center of the flower. You are ready to be responsible for this expression.

Place your heart at the Center, and keep breathing...

NORTH: WISDOM

It has been quite some time since you have seen the Master. Indeed, you wonder if that first experience ever really happened. Yet this evening, as you sit by the fire, weaving your heart-felt melody with the crackling flame, the memory comes alive. Holding the Flute in your hand, you lay down near the hearth, watching the flickering flame as your eyelids drift together. The warmth of the flames becomes the warmth of Spring's sun. Mockingbird flutters and struts before you as you walk the well-worn path. The gentle night rain has left a shimmering pool in a hollow in the rock. As you gaze into the reflecting pool, you see, once again, the face of the Master.

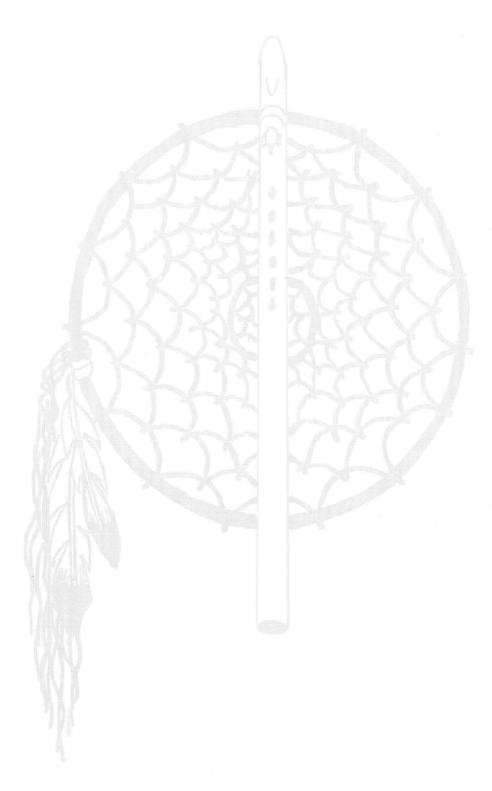

APPENDIX:

Bonus Track "Morning Dances": **39**

FLUTE ANATOMY

Here's what your flute looks like inside:

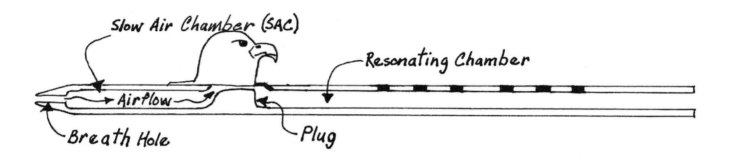

The sound or "voice" of your flute will vary according to construction and materials—types of wood.

For more information, refer to Clint Goss' excellent website, Flutopedia:
http://www.clintgoss.com/flutopedia.com/index.htm

CARE

Your Flutemaker will provide you with instructions here. Any wooden instrument should be shielded from extreme temperature fluctuations (don't leave the Flute on your dashboard on a hot sunny day!) and moisture. Extreme caution and supervision with young children and pets! Every year or two I like to swab the inside of my Flutes with almond or walnut oil and let them sit for a day or two without playing them, but many makers don't think this is necessary.

TROUBLESHOOTING

Having trouble with the sound stopping or getting weaker? After playing for a while, the air channel can swell from the moisture, or fill with water condensing from your breath. This is called "wetting up." Sometimes, you can clear the passage by blowing sharply, or you can remove the block and dry channels manually.

Another cause of weak or no sound is movement of the block—adjust and retie until you find your Flute's "sweet spot"—most often when the front edge of the block aligns with the back edge of the sound hole.

A WORD FROM THE ILLUSTRATOR

Illustrator: Tom McCune
B.S., Art Ed.; M.A.T., Art Ed
Southeast Missouri State University

I have taught and produced art professionally for 34 years. I have served as the art chair of the Fine Art Department for the Aurora R-VIII and South Iron R-VIII school districts. I taught art history, drawing, painting, photography, ceramics, sculpture, and graphic design at the junior and senior high public school level. At the college level I have taught art history, ceramics, and drawing, as well as supervised art education student teachers during their student teaching field experience.

Thank you Tom, for all your care, attention to detail and beauty, clean lines, and sleepless nights!

AFTERWORD: MY FLUTE STORY

At the Alaska Flute Circle, we often reminisce of our encounters and ever-widening experiences with the Native American Flute. Here's my Flute Story:

Back in the late 80's I was touring with a World Beat band in Logan, Utah. After the show, a wild looking mountain man introduced himself as Crazy Coyote and said he had something special he wanted me to see. We walked to a tiny, dimly lit apartment, and he handed me what looked like a broken stick. On closer examination, it proved itself to be a Native American Flute, broken off at one end. He asked me to play it for him—the instrument jumped in my hands! To this date, I do not think I have ever played any instrument with such a subtly responsive gorgeous tone.

I went about my musical life, but the breath of Crazy Coyote's Native American Flute has always sung in the back of my memory. 15 years later, my friend Neal Martin—also known as Crazy Neal, since his vast growing and flowing collection of Native American Flutes rivaled a used car salesman in numbers and variety—came by and gave me a Charles Littleleaf flame juniper Flute. We sat by the fire in the Alaskan springtime twilight, played Flutes and marveled at the sudden profusion of singing birds that gathered around us.

My approach to playing the Native American Flute developed quite differently than the other instruments I had learned over the years. As I explored the instrument like a child through improvisation in the Alaskan outdoors, I allowed it to reveal its secrets to me. I accepted and explored uses for every rich tone, whisper, warble, and squawk I could find, regardless of traditional western conceptions of "tone." Many of the free improvisation ideas I had learned through the years, especially at the New England Conservatory of Music, took hold and sank deep roots into my Native American Flute experience.

Neal introduced me to the Alaska Flute Circle. The constant seeking and musical growth among that beautiful group inspires me constantly. I witnessed how the Flute could inspire those with little musical training or background to transform themselves into profoundly expressive composers and performers.

Flute song drifted down the spine of the Rockies as I made my way down from Alaska to Missouri. In my new home in the rolling Ozark hills, warm moonlit summer nights full of cricket, owl, frog, coyote, and bellowing herds now echo to the ever-new breathings of my Heart.

Andrew has been playing and studying musical instruments since 1965. He received his Masters in Music in Third Stream Studies (Contemporary Improvisation) from the New England Conservatory of Music in 1995. Andrew lives, teaches, and performs on Native American Flute, flutes, saxophone, piano, voice, and accordion in Southwest Missouri. He teaches music classes—including Songwriting and Music of the World—at Ozarks Technical Community College in Springfield, and is the Music Minister of Christs Community Church in Buffalo.

Andrew plays Littleleaf & Stellar flutes.

Andrew's websites:
www.sitonarock.com
www.napashamusic.com
www.heartwinds.us
www.theharmonystudio.com

YouTube Channel: napashamusic

I would love to answer your questions and hear your feedback, experiences and suggestions regarding **How to Sit on a Rock**. I am also available for teaching, workshops, performances, and speaking engagements.

Please contact me at through my websites, or email andrewbishko@sitonarock.com, and send photos, videos, and/or audio of you on your rock!

NOTES

59